RECONSIDERING THE LILIES

RECONSIDERING

The *Lilies*

To Dorothy, my love

John T.

John S. Thornton

LUMINARE PRESS

WWW.LUMINAREPRESS.COM

Luminare Press
442 Charnelton St.
Eugene, OR 97401
www.luminarepress.com

LCCN: 2022916639
ISBN: 979-8-88679-102-0

A Greeting

Thank you for purchasing a copy of *Reconsidering the Lilies*.
It's your book now, and you can do whatever you
want with it. However, may I suggest that you not read
it all at once? Just read a few poems at a time. Maybe
even just one. Oh, and read them – or that one – out
loud, even if you're all alone. Get into the language and
into the rhythm and let the poem or poems sing to you.

People sometimes ask me how long it takes to write a
poem. It takes somewhere between fifteen minutes and six
weeks. (The really hard work is done at about four o'clock
in the morning or during a too-long shower.) If I have to
labor over a poem, I'm pretty sure it's too long and will have
to find a way to shorten it. After all, poetry is about letting
a few words do the work of paragraphs and pages. Some
poems just never do make the cut. I have a box full of those.

Poetry is a way of looking at the world. Nature is full
of poetry. People are full of poetry. The poet only has to
look, listen, then record it. A poem is just given to you, if, of
course, you're paying attention. The best poems use every-
day language and don't require an unabridged dictionary.

Obviously, this collection of poems is about me, what
I see and hear and feel. It's essentially autobiographical.
You may see and hear and feel things in a very different
way. Good. Write it down. Make it sing to you. Be a
poet. It doesn't have to rhyme.

Once again, thank you for taking time with this.

+John S. Thornton, Taucross Farm, Scio, Oregon

Contents

THE THEORY OF RELATIVITY

The Sun rises sooner...
The farm gets bigger...
The grass grows faster...
The fruit higher in the trees...
Everything is farther away,
Though the Milky Way seems closer...
Only my pants get longer...
But we feel taller for wanting less,
And love is quicker and truer
And feels more like play
In this shortening of years,
Of months,
Of days.

+John S. Thornton

BECOMING

What is it we've become?
And how much each other's becoming?
The frequent Baptism in coffee cups;
a chocolate croissant, broken,
the Body of Christ;
in all the talk, an utterance
hardly less than Scripture;
our imperfect love yet casting out demons;
even faltering, raising us from the dead;
and we walk through the night hand in hand
with Mary Magnified and Lazarus;
only light around us,
and this lightness within,
and deep in the throat, a lump:
the catch of gratefulness.
Ahh, the sweetness of it all;
Ahhh...lleluia.

+John S. Thornton

MOON AND FOG

There was a Super-Moon last night
  and fog.
A fair linen lay over the land;
  and, beneath, everything, it seemed, was sacred:
  trees
        and fields,
              and barns,
                    and creek,
and every silent, sleeping creature.

O Moon, O fog, linger, please, and last
  until we love the mystery of common things,
    until we love the mystery even of ourselves,
      of flesh becoming Word,
like Moon and fog, luminous and pure.

                              +John S.Thornton

THARAKAN

(In honor of the Rt. Rev. Jos Tharakan,
Bishop of Idaho)

Ever face the warm sun early on a summer day,
Eyes closed, time unwound, the world away,
You quieted, God-graced among the multitudes?
Ever let a soft breeze raise you heart-high
Into giddiness and a glowing
And the urgency to sing, at least, "Alleluia"?
Isn't it something,
This gift of being you,
This aliveness among all who live,
This hankering now to laugh, to leap,
And, above all, this sense of God-granted worth?
Such it is when you face Jos Tharakan,
His eyes like a warm sun early on a summer day,
His smile like a soft breeze lifting you heart-high,
His whole nature awaiting you,
Just you
And only.

+John S. Thornton

THE MAN AND HIS DOG

The dog is blind now,
his world
the house,
the yard,
the car's back seat,
everywhere blackness;
doesn't take long walks,
chase the ball,
jump on the bed in the morning;
bumps into things in the hallway,
still sniffs the way to his dish,
still finds the back door,
the patio, sun-soaked and silent,
so sleeps the day through,
dreams dog dreams...

The man cherishes the dog,
the companionship undiminished;
like a personal chef,
tends the dog's diet;
like a chaufeur,
drives him to the vet;
and at day's end,
gets down on his knees,
lets the dog lick his bald head,
"the popsickle" the man calls it,
a touch worthy of the Sistine Chapel,
how one gives life to the other
and the other returns it...

There is such immensity in little things.
Michaelangelo would see it.

+John S. Thornton

NINETY TWO YEARS AGO

(In honor of my wife, Janylee, on her 92nd birthday)

Ninety-two years ago
A birth in Albert Lea,
Celebrated by autumn's fireshow,
Yellow-gold strewn across the land,
Red maples starring the Minnesota daysky,
Purple leaves of dogwoods wind-whirled,
And innuendos of winter and the white.
In the small house on Summer Street,
An exultation, of mother, of father,
Lovesongs and caresses and the hustle of care,
For this bloom of their souls' embrace,
This little flower, lovely, wondrous,
Growing day to day and through the seasons,
Rooted in the sweet loam of their lives,
A modest providence, but jubilation to the skies.
Through the summers of delight,
The falls of an uncertain grace,
Gloomswept and indifferent winters,
She has never not trusted in springs,
Nor the love that heaves itself upon our hearts.

+John S. Thornton

BABUSHKA

I looked up, and there,
seated at God's right hand
an old babushka bent,
the great-great-grandmother
of the hundred million times denied Christ,
pleading with the Sorrowing One
that Love's child would be born,
cry for life again, ever again
in our rock-hewn hearts,
save us from everything unmacculate,
every word,
every weapon,
everything that wastes us,
wastes others
and worlds,
would even walk on the flowers
among the rubble we've made.

+John S. Thornton

UVALDE

Now everybody's talking,
Pointing fingers, blaming,
Shrill and righteous,
But for those who only weep,
Wonder the why of it.
Amerie neither wonders nor weeps,
Has not one word to say,
For she lies deep in the sandy soil of South Texas,
She and twenty others, slain:
Uziyah, Nevaeh, Xavier, Makenna, Jose, Jackie,
Eliahna, Jayce, Maranda, Tess, Rojelio, Alithia,
Alexandria, Maite, Annabelle, Layla, Jailah, Eva,
Eliahana, Irma.
Stones call out their names in the night,
Only an eastwind troubles the elms and the ash,
Mute the phlox, the mallow flowering the graves,
And a cold silence in the waning moon,
Nothing in nature absolves our sacrifices to America's
Molech,
To a reckless creed, to this license we claim liberty,
To an industry for killing, killing,
Even of our children,
Even of ourselves,
For our childlikeness lies deep in the sandy soil of
South Texas
As Amerie.

+John S. Thornton

15

HIGHLAND PARK

She only wanted to see Uncle Sam on stilts,
That stovepipe hat towering the newday sky,
The marching bands, the drum majors, twirlers,
Teenage girls, upright and easy, on the palomino
posse,
Fire engines, in long line, polished redder than fire,
The mayor smiling, saluting from the dealer's
convertible,
And feel the beat of John Philip Sousa in her feet,
Feel "stars and stripes forever" in her feet.
All along the way, people sang for what was,
This dream of liberty's "sweet land" and love,
When shots rang out from a rooftop,
Proclaiming the Fourth of Apocalypse,
Bodies in the street, blood;
Everywhere the wounded, old people, toddlers,
And a universal howl, now still a weeping,
This weariness of what, by law, we've sanctioned.
"This is not freedom," the woman said.
This is not freedom.

+John S. Thornton

17

MAUNDY THURSDAY

These feet are mine,
Nearly ninety now,
Formed in my mother's womb,
Kicked the time to be in this world.
She washed them, dried them,
Tweaked each toe, one, two, three...;
Foot upon foot, kissed a canticle for me.
Of course, I don't remember it;
But how can love's logic ever be forgotten?

Tonight, I'll wash others' feet.
Barefoot, modest, they'll step the stairs,
Sit, put their feet in the warm, soapy basin.
And I, for the Mother God, will wash them,
Slowly dry, slowly anoint, kiss them.
Though few seem lovely,
All are beautiful,
For upon them the Christ may stand,
Upon them may walk this world
With all the poor in spirit,
The stride of those who will love.

+John S. Thornton

THE AEROBAT

Silver-winged, he drifted there
among the early morning sunrays
golding the sky above the fields,
the wheat, the rye grass greening,
houses shadowed by the mountain
and silent...
But then, full-throttled, thrilled,
he barrel-rolled and -rolled – and
rolled us out of bed and to the window,
now eyes believing ears,
an aerobat dancing on the air...
and, then, a loop-the-loop, another,
and another before he dizzily dove
straight down, field- and houseward,
screaming a carnival scream, and,
at an instant, turned, climbed straight up,
engine roaring "Hurray," and
floated again on the sunrays of morning,
soon was gone on thin sound and
silence...
and we, aroused, awake now,
as if startled by an archangel silver-winged,
resolved to rise and roar "Hurray" each day
for sky and fields and,
though grounded,
these aerobatic lives we live
awhile.

+John S. Thornton

PORK

The slaughter house is closed – for now.
Covid-19 palls this place on the Prairie;
Only the falls break the Sioux Falls silence;
Unwearying waters sing to the sad city.
(Pray the river never runs dry – and the song.)
Today, ten thousand pigs are reprieved,
As ten thousand yesterday,
Ten thousand tomorrow again.
No squeals will gather to a curdling shriek,
Like thunder rumbling, rolling over the Plain,
Darkening, deafening predation's sight and sound.
Like the animals we sacrifice,
Prodded, we too are caught up, hung,
Moved along in this mechanism of death,
Sabbath-less and unsorrowing,
Valuing little; all things lesser than we;
Fed and fat, our humanity is wasting;
This fury now must be Mother Earth's,
Must be mad, crying for her children,
That once again we'll wonder,
Once again feel all hallowed
Beneath our feet,
Above our heads,
Soil and sky,
All that lives between.

+John S. Thornton

THE HARMONICA PLAYER

He sat on the sidewalk, a large man,
leaned against a dress shop window,
shirted in yesterdays, trousered
in neglect and aloneness, sad shoes
from the worried wandering for food,
a bed, the worth of his existence,
a bowler downside-up for dollars, dimes,
eyes closed, seeing maybe a symphony,
and played his harmonica, breathed
such beauty that mannequins, clothed
in poppies, seemed transfixed.
People stopped, stood, felt the music
as if within themselves, the street corner
a concert hall, a peace beyond all pain.
A while, we put money in the hat,
walked away with the moment's immensity
and looked back at the man making music
and the mannequins clothed in poppies
and the people stopped
to start again,
this time lilting,
maybe loving.

+John S. Thornton

EARTHWORMS

"You can grow corn in cinders," he said,
"If you have enough fertilizer."
— A Nebraska farmer

Walk through our pasture some day, Sunshown,
Silent, but for a westwind's whisper,
The ryegrass, timothy softly switching your shins,
Slowing your impetuous pace, calling your attention
To what's low and rambunctious, the sprawling
White clover - or the red - and a random patch
Of wild iris, star-shaped and shining, as if the night sky
Were under your feet, and everywhere dandelions
Wild and tipsy, and you drunk with adoration,
and your self rooted deep in surrender and...
Laughter.

Kneel now, as before a sacred thing.
Lie on your back,
You the grasses, the clover, the wild iris, dandelions;
You the Sun, clouds swinging on the mirth of air;
You the westwind whispering the language heart-
heard;
You one with all that's wonderous, all offered you.
Roll over on your belly now,
Put your ear against the ground.
Can you hear it?
Can you hear the music of the soil-makers,
The continual anthems of earthworms, of beetles,
Moles and the millions microscopic beneath

The form of you, the form of us all,
Making a sacrament as common as dirt
For all who walk through the greenness,
All who lie gladly upon the grasses?

If anyone asks what you're doing, say,
I'm loving the Earth,
Earthworms and all.

+John S. Thornton

KETANJI

(In honor of Ketanji Brown Jackson, Associate Justice,
United States Supreme Court)

The Capitol police escorted her,
As if a priceless gem,
That sapphire woman,
That emerald,
That ruby,
That diamond,
Every facet of her a radiance,
Her eyes, listening as she looked,
Her smile, fearless of upbraid or adulation,
Every word from the deep well of learning the Law,
And a settled law of love in her life.
However...
Some will not love the less of themselves,
Four White men,
One White woman,
All senators from old slave states,
Formed in ways that deform them now,
So see her in the dark.
She who lives in brightness
Would only illumine them.

+John S. Thornton

29

NELA

(In memory of Cornelia Wattley)

Once each year,
sometimes twice,
even a third time,
she'd Chevy herself to paradise -
or just this side of it –
Yosemite-bound, a blue streak down I-5,
Awhanhee hardly noticed
nor yearned,
to a place richer than luxury,
Tuolumne Meadows.
She'd unfurl a tarp
among a whimsy of wildflowers,
sleeping bag rolled out,
then sleep – the night drifting dreamily
star to star.
In the morning,
as Sun ascended the mountain,
she'd lie wrapped in a gauze
of ground fog, damp
in baptismal dew, strewn
like wet diamonds,
a new being
among all that was new in a day,
Nature still sculpting, still painting,
and always singing,
singing as the winds,
as the waters,

singing as the tiny Tanagers,
and her heart sang too,
the song called
>Ooooh!

+John S. Thornton

THE HOUSE WREN

Each day,
in the mornng light
lazy among the maples,
a tiny House Wren,
less than half the size of my hand,
hardly heavier than its feathers,
perched on the deck railing,
trilling...trilling...trilling...
its breast bulging like a bellows,
its head skyward,
its beak wide open
as if an aria of tragic love,
for us at table beyond the glass door,
perhaps a Pavoratti among the birds.
But there seemed something so insistent,
something that felt like a scolding,
even a scathing
from this tiny bird,
this tiny body of vehemence,
as if Ezekiel, a prophet on the railing,
warning us to change our ways,
else none will live
to see the morning light
lazy among the maples.

+John S. Thornton

ALL IN WHITE SHE WAS

Softly, the music played.
They came into the room,
She in his arms.
He set her there,
His bride,
As if an angel in the winged chair.
All in white she was,
Calm and candlelit,
Luminous within,
A woman ravaged by m. s.,
Defying now the darkness, death
This night of her wedding,
The groom at her side.
Since childhood best friends,
But married others,
Divorced.
Then returned that long love,
And with it a plea,
That, with a vow, he'd be father to her sons.
"I take thee to my wedded Wife,
To have and to hold from this day forward...
Till death us do part...."
And death did,
Soon parted them.
At the grave, father and sons spoke of an angel,
All in white she was,
Luminous within.

+John S. Thornton

ANDREW

(In memory of my father,
Andrew Robertson Thornton)

It was there,
on the desk
in the guest room,
propped against the wall,
a photograph of my father,
a young man,
lanquid smile,
not suppressing hilarity,
for none was in him,
ever,
maybe an emerging thankfulness,
home from the war in Europe,
from Verdun and the trenches,
uninjured, though gassed,
yet a war-wounded soul,
expecting little from human beings,
less from their God;
but, half-smiling,
lucky to be alive
and to have met the young woman
who would become my mother.
For seven years of my life he lived,
ag teacher and basketball coach,
I tagging behind,
classroom to gym to farms,
he uttering quietness...and gentleness...

and something far away...
I can't remember a thing he ever said,
nor the sound of his voice.
I remember only that guttural groan
as the doctor pounded his chest,
a gurgle
and a silence deep as death
as he whom I adored fled
into the winter night,
leaving a lifeless body behind
and me, uncomprehending.
Eighty years later,
I wonder if, somehow, he still breathes
in me
as I, somehow, must breathe in my son,
all ruffling the air
and a single utterance of decency.

+John S. Thornton

WILLIAM

(In honor of Bill Neel, Eugene, Oregon)

Looking back, you'll see
the architecture of his soul.

You'll see
a boy, a youth become a man
living life as he would live it,
never an imitation of another,
unafraid and fresh and free.

   You'll see
   such a love of learning,
   an impassioned pursuit of fact;
   and, once knowing, such a settling
   and the ordering of action.

You'll see
him at his drawing,
an artist's eye for loveliness,
an engineer's for endurance,
in everything a mastery
for a heart's habitation.

   You'll see
   a liberality with wealth –
   and a liberality with words! –
   though in friendship the greatest riches
   as in the weal of a worn prayer book.

You'll see
a man who lives in the West,
the West, hat and boots, in him,
groomed mules and lustrous wagon,
Lyn, the form of grace for him, along,
together bearing the wonder of the past,
together bearing the romance of the present.

Looking back, you'll see
the architecture of his soul.

+John S. Thornton

RETICENCE

By moonlight, I saw the fields frozen,
all immobile as the grasses,
all silent as their silvering,
elk not shuffling through the apples,
nor coyotes calling from the hills,
wild turkeys still among the trees,
and we unspeaking before the sun.
Wordless, a sooth is saying:
the world heals as voices cease,
but for geese gathering in the creek,
Barred Rocks rustling the roost,
and my stroke of the cat on the couch.
One day, we'll long for reticence,
speak only what's worded by the heart
and gaze, muted, at such goodness
as is all about us
and in you.

+John S. Thornton

FITZ-GERALD

(In honor of Greg Fitz-Gerald, Eugene, Oregon)

You'd think it a grizzly
coming at you,
growling –
but it's Greg,
clawless and kindly,
wishing only to engage you,
mind and spirit,
his heart bigger than Kansas,
to the beat of ancestral Ireland.
He's like a kid at a carnival
in a tilt-a-whirl world,
everything eye-popping,
everything breath-taking,
everything screaming "whee,"
everything for life's enlargement.
He'll go east
and he'll go west
and nothing's foreign,
except people's unwonder.
He'll see glory's flash or flicker
in little things,
Monet in a Thai dish,
Michelangelo in smoke's curling,
and, in the human face,
the lineament of laughter
or the lines of pain,
always a pieta in mother and child.

And the whole wide world contracted
in home
and in the heart of his beloved,
Susan.

+John S. Thornton

THE TATTOOED TELLER

The teller is tattooed.
Rosalie is, let me tell you.
She's new to the bank.
Pretty young woman.
Very friendly.
Efficient.
I'd seen her several times before,
but never so much of her as today.
Above the low neckline of her blouse,
I could see--
couldn't help but see –
the tips of wings tattooed to her chest.
Of an eagle?
Of an angel?
Did I ask?
Of course, I didn't ask!
Only an oaf would ask!
But my mind took flight,
fluttered as she counted cash,
soared like a dream in adolescence.
I thanked her,
very much,
for her services,
and winged away.

In the car, I told my wife.
She rolled her eyes.
 "You'll come back to earth," she said.

I still wonder if
it's an eagle
or an angel.

+John S. Thornton

HERE

Soon,
Lessons of love are learned,
The tenderness,
The terror
Of the wondering heart.
The boy,
Mothered to apprehend angels,
Beheld the startling presence
In his own classroom,
Bright as the mid-day sun,
Soft as moonlight and tranquil,
Deep as a sweet well of water,
The whole nature of her rare,
Rare and good,
Like an angel fallen from his heaven.
He felt such a betrothal
That it had to be announced:
Bought a blue necklace,
He and his mother;
Handed it to the angel in the hallway,
"Here," he said, otherwise wordless,
By love befuddled.
"Here I am," is what he meant,
The boy before an angel who can't be caught,
Headed now for other heavens,
Of books and basketballs
And a sky blue with futures;
But some day distant,
Blue necklace in hand,

A boy will say, "Here I am,"
And she'll say,
"Here I am"
Too.

+John S. Thornton

MAGI

Suppose they were the Magi,
not on camels coming,
nor coming from the east,
neither kings of any kind.

They come from the south,
following a star in the north,
dressed, shod in charities,
bathed in dust, in dirt,
bearing neither frankincense
nor myrrh,
nor pockets full of pesos,
only themselves,
like gold,
refined in the crucible
  of poverty,
    of violence,
      of death's indifference,
the purification of a courage to be,
alive and seeking always so,
labor and hunger's satisfactions,
and the dove's descent with peace
in a land where the Christ Child cries.

At the river,
another Herod has built a wall,
high and heralding hatred,
and beyond,
the Christ Child's cry is distant,

less even than an echo;
but One awaits *that moment* when
all the greathearted shout, roar
like Joshua and the tribes at Jericho,
and the wall tumbles down,
and the Magi wade
  into our welcome
    (and into our shame).

+John S. Thornton

CHARLEY+

(In honor of Charley+ and Diane Burger,
Boise, Idaho)

You'd think it a wand waved for the magic he works,
But it's the walking stick he swings, stomps,
Vaults himself to your embrace,
As if in flight on a whisp of whimsy,
Bows to the you in the deepest depth of you,
Lifts you on laughter from doubt to daring,
From the fears that leave you half-alive,
Now you wondrous and two-thirds wild.
Sure, he's an old man now,
Yesterdays far more than tomorrows,
But this day is the birthday of all his births,
Each word a gust for blowing out candles
And singing some old untiring song.
He knows sickness, knows injury too,
Knows how to wait, wait upon the healing,
For there is rising in his marrow.
Darkness will never engulf him.
He lives in the sun's light,
Eats with her,
Sleeps with her,
She the sun who never sets,
With her bears a banner which proclaims
OF LOVE BE NOT ASHAMED.

+John S. Thornton

THE PITCHER

The boy in the baggy pants loped to the mound,
A cap snagged on a thicket of wild hair,
He hardly wider than, as they say, a rail,
Nor weighing much more than a bag of bats,
Seemed elsewhere and airy on the day's soft breeze.
Batters saw balls like moons beyond the bleachers,
Clapping against the concrete of the street called Glee.
Batter up!, the umpire yelled.
Up he came on the music of cleats, casual, confident.
The pitcher wound up, mind and muscles twisted into
a tornado,
From hand to catcher's mitt, the ball only a blur,
A fastball right down the middle of the batter's triple
dream.
Strike!!!
At the closing, three batters went dizzily to the
dugout;
Ten pitches, fastballs, sliders, sinkers, curves spun
them.
And the boy in the baggy pants kicked a little Bolshoi
kick,
The language of baseball's ballet,
And the rhetoric of one who speaks in knuckleballs.

+John S. Thornton

"TEDDY"

(in honor of Ted Berktold+, Eugene, Oregon)

Around the furniture
he'll come, rambling,
bow-legged under the weight
of an unabridged exuberance,
a sin, he'd say, to sqaunder
a single moment in this world,
every day another Big Bang,
stars flying about him,
a galaxy of gladness,
beauty all the way from Penny
to the edge of wonder,
so take you, laureate or refugee,
into his voluble, uproarious self
and imagine you God's messenger.

He'll tell about growing up in Minnesota,
a farm snow-swept in long, lonely winters,
sun-blistered day to darkness in summers,
father, mother, nine children,
feeding chickens,
slopping pigs,
shoveling manure –
all the while feeling a Voice calling him,
calling, calling, calling him beyond corn,
to a different planting,
to a different harvest,
and he was gone.

A priest he's been these decades,
five now or more.
He's been faithful
and skilled
and tireless
and serious too –
but in everything that isn't tragic
he'll see something essentially comical
about our race,
always as smart as St. Paul,
always as funny as Jonathan Winters.

+John S. Thornton

THE DERMATOLOGIST

Like the sun slipping around
the mountain in the morning,
the dermatologist slips around
the half-opened door, rayed
on strawberry shoes, a smile
chasing all darknesses away,
talks, laughs, beams...
bends, gazes, once again,
does what needs to be done,
does it,
      swift
       and sure
       and mirthful,
a man whose work seems sacred play,
breaking, say, into lithe alleluias...

then, on strawberry shoes, leaves
lightly, like the full moon leaves
at the sunning of the day
and a warmth as I go.

+John S. Thornton

COCONUT CREAM PIE

Tuckered out, the Lord thought it best
to take a long break, get a good rest.
In Peter's boat, he sailed the Geneseret;
dozed a while, not a worry, not a fret.
However....
Folks learned where he'd be landing,
circled the lake in hope of glad-handing.
When at last he disembarked,
it was getting late, getting darked.
Everyone was hungry, Abigails and Hermans;
it was time for some food, not for sermons.
But....
There were just three wee fish and seven *artous*.
Now this may sound odd and awfully abstruse:
artous is "bread" – or "cake" – or coconut cream pie!
O my, that pie made the Lord levitate and fly.
He took those seven pies and cut them in pieces,
each into seven hundred, right on the beaches.
Five thousand people had only one little bite,
but they felt raised up to heaven's high height,
all with those yummy coconut cream pies,
just seven of them, and that's no lies.
That's why they say, in tones that are spherical,
that coconut cream pie is some kind of miracle.

+John S. Thornton

EDEN

Eden is a narrow place,
The size of each man's soul,
Each woman's too.
Only two trees there,
Both luxuriant,
Both ample;
The fruit of one sweet,
Always sweetening;
The other, the opposite, bitter,
Ever bittering.
In between a hammock's hung,
Where humanity swings,
Side to side,
Heaven's above,
Teased and tested,
Sunup to -down and in their sleep.
All our ancestors warned us –
And theirs before them –
Since Adam and Eve swung there,
That our souls forbid the bitter fruit.
A Voice says,
Don't eat that fruit!
You'll regret it!
Believe me!
But we say,
We'll see for ourselves.
It couldn't be that bitter.
Nobody's going to tell us what to do.
Like the pips of an apple,

We're spit out of Eden,
On our asses in a patch of dust,
Wondering how in hell to make a garden of it,
Angels glowering,
Eyes like flaming swords.
The myth keeps repeating itself,
For we keep thinking we're gods,
Know everything
But our own hearts
And humility
Ample and luxuriant.

+John S. Thornton

THE ACORN

It was a sound,
like castanets,
that awakened us,
a mariachi in the tree...

then
another,
as if a train,
whistling,
were racing through
on the way to sunrise...

then
that crash,
that shattering,
that jangle,
that rolling, rolling
into an eerie hush
and wonder...

and we
sat straight up,
on the edge of terror,
to see that the old oak had,
in a single moment,
thunderclapped all its acorns
against the yearning earth,
that the planet,
appealing to Nature,

shall not be unfutured,
that our swarming race
will see our hope
in an acorn,
dying,
to rise in the spring
and greening.

+John S. Thornton

THE WEDDED ONE

(for a woman grieving)

For love,
she spent herself,
body spent,
      mind spent,
            spirit spent
during the days of his dying;
then she herself died
a momentary death,
an awful emptiness
as if the grave – but
awoke,
      arose,
           lives still,
willed by him to do and to be,
by her own willing to become,
all the while the two of them one,
his wedding ring against her breast.

+John S. Thornton

THE MULTI-COLORED COAT

We could see, in the distance, a multi-colored coat;
Closer, see a small boy buttoned up within,
Wool cap pulled down over his eyebrows and ears,
Mittens big as boxing gloves for a fight for life,
Boots buckled against that winter of war,
That snow, that ice and a future frozen,
Kicking stones as if each a Russian soldier,
Looking back for father, bawling,
Ahead for mother, bawling the more,
Neither brother nor sister seeking him
Along this road from Kyiv to wherever humanity
lives,
Or even death unnoticed among the multitude dying.
You ask the boy's name?
His name?
His name is "Christ,"
A name defamed by those who once proclaimed his
love,
Would now, for power, casually crucify him.

+John S. Thornton

DESSERT

"Oh, John," she said,
(my wife)
"you are dessert!"
"Dessert," I asked,
"like
the Mars Bars mousse in Wales...
the citrus tapioca pudding in France...
the Euphoria hot fudge sundaes in Eugene...
your own rhubarb meringue pie?"
"Better," she said,
"better than them all."
An old man now, I'm just a metaphor:
I'm mousse,
I'm pudding,
a hot fudge sundae
and pie.
Even when I'm sour,
she calls me confected,
a sweetness at the end of this feast;
but I remember when I was the entree
and would love to be the entree again –
and the hors d'oeuvre too –
now *that* was the consumate feast.

+John S. Thornton

THE CANE

At ninety-two, she takes my arm.
It's a s-l-o-w dance we do.
Mendelssohn is in our step.
"Here comes," arm-in-arm,
Still bride, groom are we.
Now she carries a cane too.
It's more a march we do.
"Yankee Doodle" is in our feet
And laughter every exhalation.
Old love is renewed on silly song,
A daring defines our days
As we vault ourselves along,
Her cane a drum major's mace,
She the leader, I the led
In this ramble of a parade.

+John S. Thornton

DIESEL

To fill the tank with diesel,
I drive the tractor to Lacomb.
It's uphill all the way,
Down all the way back;
The sun warms my cheeks in spring;
In winter, cold westwinds weep my nose .
At eight miles an hour, I watch the Earth dying,
Then rising, spendthrift again and whimsical.
Today, wheat fields are plowed and fallowed,
The blueberry bushes barren and brittle,
But hazelnuts insisting to be swept,
Row after row along this verdant valley,
And here, at our house, apples now, pears to pick.
Oh, this rhythm, this rhyme of endings, of
beginnings,
My heart full of exclamations –
Though during these burnt weeks I wonder
If Earth will grudge so much miraculous,
Tire of our swarm and our dominion,
I, latest to this land,
This gift of glaciers,
               of Calapooias
                    of pioneers
and millions of earth-makers unseen.

+John S. Thornton

RECONSIDERING THE LILIES

Reader:
You have to see it,
That one daylily
Apart from all the others.
See it in every light;
See it in the morning
As the long, low rays lift it skyward;
Again at mid-day
As the sun sets it, petal by petal, aflame;
And in the evening
As the shadows slowly darken the day.

Audience:
Only then,
From its bloom to its withering,
Do you see its singularity;
Only then,
All that is rare about it,
All that is beautiful.

Reader:
You have to see it,
That one daylily
Apart from all the others.
See if from every angle;
From the front porch,
As if upon a fallen star;
Alongside,
A companion in the ease and effort of creation;

And on your knees,
Setting it free from weeds that waste it.

Audience:
Only then,
From its bloom to its withering,
Do you see its singularity;
Only then,
All that is rare about it,
All that is beautiful.

Reader:
With all of us,
With you,
With me,
Time must be taken.
See us in every light;
See us from every angle,
From our bloom to our withering.
Only then can be seen our singularity,

Audience:
Only then,
All that is rare about us,
All that is beautiful.

+John S. Thornton

Acknowledgements

Of course, the author gets his name on the cover—and all the poems are his—but it takes a lot of people to make a book. We live by other people's competencies and collaboration.

I think of my sister-in-law, Joline DeJong, who lives in Pella, Iowa. Joline did the painting of the lilies on the cover of the book. She's one of Iowa's celebrated landscape painters. Though long since retired, Joline was on the faculty of Central College, that beautiful small college in Pella, for many years. She remains beloved by her former students and colleagues—and more than them all, by her sister, my wife, Janylee, and me. Her painting is a gift. Her whole life is.

The original cover of the book, slightly modified by the publisher, was done by Roger Gaither, who, literally, lives just down the road, in the little town of Scio, Oregon. Roger is always swift to respond to appeals for help (and swift to complete a task). Roger has spent a lifetime as a graphic artist, in academia and private business. His talent is extraordinary. Roger and his wife, May Garland, are models of community activism. Democracy is one of their highest values.

Finally, I want to thank the Luminare Press. Every encounter with their staff is full of assurance and light-heartedness. You leave knowing that they'll fulfill your highest expectations.

+John S. Thornton